There's A Party In The Pit...
and You're Invited

~~~~~~~~~~

LEARNING TO LIVE IN THE LIGHT WHEN IT'S STILL SO DARK

Dear Judy –
Your Dreams have become a beautiful reality!
Thank You for sharing your gifts and talents! :)
Blessings –
Joy

Joy Ware Miller

REFERENCE

What Others' Are Saying. . .

* Joy Ware Miller's book addressing how faith can allow one to heal from the greatest loss anyone can imagine-that of one's child-is heartwarming and inspiring indeed. Her faith in God is palpable, real, contagious. Like the author, the book is filled with the kind of faith that allows one to continue to go on living fully and to continue to believe in one's God despite almost unbearable pain.
~Cheryl Fenno, Ph.D., Dean, College of Arts & Sciences, Urbana University

*This book will change your life. Joy's story is heart wrenching, but the words of her triumphant journey have the power to provide comfort to the brokenhearted, hope for those who mourn, and freedom to the captives of despair. Joy intimately and transparently walks readers through the power of finding purpose and perspective after tragedy. "There's A Party In The Pit...and You're Invited" will reignite your passion, inspire your heart, and revive your soul. I highly recommend it for anyone desperate for breakthrough and transformation. ~ Anna Quesada Founder & President, Christian Women's Small Business Association

*This book is simple yet profound in its approach to healing a hurting heart. "There's a Party in the Pit" offers practical and spiritual solutions to grief and loss of any kind. A must read for those dealing with loss, especially the loss of a loved one. ~Thalia Williams, CEO, Sophia Research Consulting, LLC.

*Joy lovingly shares her story and how her faith carried her through and allowed her to live to party not only in the pit but outside the pit. Through her prayerful, heartfelt word art, Joy shares hope, inspiration and her love. A must read for anyone who is in a life pit and needs a lift up and out. ~ Patsy Foxworth Business Coach, Foxworth Consulting Group, President, National Association of Women Business Owners San Antonio Chapter, Senior Partner, Confidential Search Solutions

DEDICATED. . .

I dedicate this book to all of those who have struggled or still

struggle to live in the light, when it is still so dark!

My prayers are with you, as you read this book. . .

SPECIAL THANK YOU...

I wanted to give a Special Thank You to all of my friends and family

who have walked this journey with me! Your love and support

continues to change my life.

Thank you Dr. Cheryl Fenno, friends and family for your

editing guidance.

My parents, John and Joan Ware, have been my rock...thank you!

A Precious Shout-out to my dear Husband, Charles, my daughters

Lauren and Olivia, and my son, Christopher, I will see you again. . .

There's A Party In The Pit

There's a party in the pit
You're invited to come along
Experience mayhem and confusion
You can sing sad depressing songs.

The songs of grief, despair and hopelessness,
Of strife and pain and fear.
Sleepless nights and restless days
Filled with memories and many tears.

But wait the party has begun…
In the midst of how I feel,
It's not based upon emotions, but
A God that's mighty real.

Real through all the tribulation,
The doubt, the fear and unbelief
The God who lifts your head
When you are wrecked with so much grief.

A party in the pit?
When you are feeling very sad?
A party in the pit?
When your dreams are all but gone?
A party in the pit?
When life has treated you so wrong?
Yes…
A party in the pit
Not based upon circumstance

But a God who gives you a second, third, fourth, fifth, sixth and
seventh chance…

A party in the pit
Not based upon who you are
Not the clothes you wear or your fancy car,
But because of whose you are.
Yes…
A party in the pit
You hear music in the air?
The Word of God giving life
And so much of His love to share
Yes…
A party in the pit
And being strengthened by the load
Gaining character, faith and fortitude
In each bump along the road
Yes…
To party in the pit, difficult you say?
That's right, but not impossible
God will direct and show you the way.

It was the Pit, and tough times bringing me to my knees
Trusting God, standing in faith
When there was nothing I could see.

A party in the pit
Like Paul learned to rejoice
Accepting the same invitation
And that will be my choice.

Please RSVP to the "Party In The Pit"!

CONTENTS:

CHAPTER ONE

Where's The Party?

Because This Is The Pits

I must not think it strange if God takes in youth those whom I would have kept on earth until they were older. God is peopling eternity, and I must not restrict Him to old men and women.

Jim Elliot (1927-1956)

~ ~ ~ ~ ~

At the hospital, I remember hearing Christopher's first cry and holding him close in my arms. He was our first born, such a beautiful baby with a full head of dark black hair. I was recognized on that wing as the Mother with the baby with all that hair!

I looked into his eyes and knew we had so much time…the future was ahead of us. I could envision Christopher's first steps, learning how to ride a bike, going to school, growing and enjoying friends. However, our first order of business was thanking the Lord and dedicating him back to God. We were all together to party and celebrate Christopher's arrival.

Soon after Christopher, came Lauren, then Matthew. However, we only had the opportunity to see Matthew on an ultra-sound picture and hear his heart beat once. His heart stopped beating at sixteen weeks into the pregnancy. Life had started and ended so quickly in the womb. We were all devastated and disappointed that Matthew would not grow up with us here. Olivia arrived three years later bringing up the rear. Looking back, it seemed like we had so much time…and the future was ahead of us.

At an early age, all three children, Christopher, Lauren and Olivia asked Jesus into their hearts. We felt as parents, it was our responsibility to introduce them to Christ and train them in the way of the Word. The children loved Jesus and loved hearing Bible stories. Christopher was fascinated with Heaven and always wanted to know more. Heaven was and still is a wonderful topic for our family. We would dream about the activities and what we would see when we get there. We would debate who was going to ask Jesus the real, hard, deeper questions…like what's your last name?

Our family was just like any other family. We were active in church, with our family and our jobs. The children were involved with sports, riding horses, blowing bubbles in the back yard and being wonderful kids. We loved to go on vacations…but it was a rare thing because we didn't have a lot of extra cash. So we would walk, ride bikes and do things close to home. The best thing was the ice-cream runs after a hot summer day. We loved to party and celebrate being together. It seemed like we had so much time… and the future was ahead of us.

Christopher always loved pretending to have supernatural strength and abilities. At one time as younger children, he had Lauren believing he had made her invisible. That game only lasted until she walked in front of the mirror and could still see herself. He was always rescuing the weak or those who were afraid to fight. He had a deep desire to rescue the perishing and be a defender of good versus evil.

As Christopher began to reach his teens…he was growing at an amazing pace. I remember him patting me on my head and telling me that I was such a little thing. He had already shot past me...and was looking at his Dad eye to eye. He started playing basketball and loved the sport. He was known as the gentle giant off the court and nick-named the beast on the court. He had his eyes set on heading toward the NBA and many of us thought that was a real possibility. It seemed like we had so much time...and the future was ahead of us, but time was actually running out.

Life In The Pit

Thirteen years later, at the hospital again, I now hear the doctor say, "Mr. and Mrs. Miller, we're sorry, we have done all we can do." Our precious thirteen-year-old son lay motionless on a thin metal bed in a small emergency room. The absolute perfect picture of health we thought. Just two hours ago, Christopher had left to play basketball at the YMCA and our lives were normal. Then we received an alarming telephone call that we will never forget. "Christopher has collapsed, he is not conscious and the paramedics are on their way." Immediately, my husband and I were on our way to the YMCA. Many thoughts started to race through my head. It seemed like I was praying on automatic pilot. I knew the Word, believed the Word and was claiming scripture out loud. My husband kept saying "stay in faith." That ten-minute drive took only about five minutes that day, but felt like an eternity.

We ran from our car past the ambulance to see our son surrounded by at least six desperately focused and hardworking paramedics. They were anxiously working on Christopher to stabilize him and move him to the nearby hospital. Care-flight was standing by; however, Christopher was not responding. Finally, they transported him to the hospital and were able to get his heart beating a couple of times…but could not keep it going. Finally, after forty-five long agonizing minutes of praying and waiting outside the Emergency Room, we were summoned into the room where they were working on Christopher.

We couldn't wait to talk with him and see how he was doing, and find out exactly what happened. The paramedics, nurses and technicians stood back as we entered the very still room and confronted the soft yet deafening sound of the heart monitor with a flat steady line. We saw what no parent wants to see and we were told what no parent wants to hear. The doctor said, "Mr. and Mrs. Miller, we are sorry; we have done all we can do." The room was silent and very somber. It was as if time stood still. I didn't even know if my next breath would come. My heart sank and my feet felt like bricks. I was frozen for a moment, absorbing the words I was hearing and seeing my son so motionless. My mind flashed back to the hospital and holding Christopher as a baby. Where had the time gone? What did our future hold now?

However, even in the midst of our deepest sorrow, I could sense the unsurpassed peace and presence of God. I knew God had to be real. For me to stand at the side of my first born and watch our dreams fade – to feel his body become cold and see no life in his eyes and not go crazy…I absolutely knew God was real. I leaned down and whispered in my precious son's ear…"I love you and I will see you soon." Two thoughts ran through my mind at that time.

One was "…to be absent from the body is to be present with the Lord" (2 Corinthians 5:8). My other thought was "God, you are a good God" (Mark 10:18). *But how could He be good?* We were looking at our thirteen-year-old son lying lifeless on a sterile hospital gurney. The heart monitor that should be showing a strong heart-beat with an up and down rhythm was showing a continuous flat line.

The American Heart Association, Journal Report, 2004 stated "Hypertrophic Cardiomyopathy occurs in about one in 500 people in the general population, and it is the most common cause of sudden death in young people." Hypertrophic Cardiomyopathy (HCM) is an excessive thickening of the heart muscle. The thickening makes it harder for blood to leave the heart, forcing the heart to work harder to pump blood.

Why was my son the one out of 500? Could it be, that my son's life would be the one that would eventually affect even more than 500? It was all in God's hands, even though I had many questions and felt like I was in the *Pit* of despair, depression and discouragement.

We may experience despair, discouragement, heartache and hurts in this life on earth, but our God has promised us a new life, a restored life with Him in Heaven (Revelations 21:4). When the bottom of your world falls out…it is natural to ask why. Why did this happen? Why did God allow this to happen?

It seemed like now…time was standing still and the future was irrelevant. We were in the midst of experiencing God's goodness. Yes, I said, we were experiencing God's goodness. In that emergency room on March 10, 2005, we experienced the worst possible scenario of losing our son to a physical death. However, in the face of death, we could sense God's awesome presence in that room and His promise to be with us, helping us, comforting us and supernaturally taking the blow, the brunt of the impact of the separation of our first child. We were experiencing God's goodness, not based upon our circumstances that were unfolding before our eyes, but from God's promise to be with us when we face disappointment, heartache and tragedy.

Now let me explain, why I say we were experiencing God's

goodness in the midst of such a devastating unexpected tragedy. For the last seven years to the exact date of Christopher's physical death on March 10, 2005, I had been learning about God's goodness. On March 10, 1998, I had the miscarriage with Matthew. I was very angry and distraught at that time and could not understand if God is a good God...how could He let my baby die?

I had grown up loving God and really felt like He let me down. Why would He allow me to go through such a desperately dark time? I was angry, sad and had many questions for God. Hindsight would prove how God was grooming my heart for those seven years even through the pain. We reluctantly had to leave the hospital to go home to tell our two young girls, Lauren 10 and Olivia 5, their big brother was not coming home.

The slow drive home was much different than the high-speed pursuit to the YMCA. My precious friend Betty had been watching the girls and keeping them occupied, knowing that Christopher died, yet not telling them – waiting for us to be there to gently break the news. Where do you begin? The girls are thinking, maybe he broke his arm or sprained his ankle. Their eyes penetrated into ours and we grabbed them and held them tight. We said, "your brother is with Jesus." "He is not coming home."

Those words just hung in the air, to be shattered only by Lauren's gut wrenching scream. She ran out of the house screaming and could not stop shaking. Olivia was still so young…she didn't quite capture the depth of what was happening. March 10, 2005 changed our *normal* lives forever.

Learning In The Pit

I had served God from a very early age, growing up a *PK* (Pastor's Kid) and loving God with all my heart. How could my 13-year-old son die? Couldn't God take better care of us than that? I realized unfortunate things could happen, but not tragedies, not to me! I felt like God had let me down again and that I could no longer trust Him. When I had the miscarriage seven years prior to Christopher's physical death, I kept asking God, "if you are a good God…why did you let my baby die?" I never got the answer to why, but I did find out more about God's goodness.

I continued going to church, even though I did not feel like going. I would sit at church and feel numb. It seemed like everyone was so happy. Seeing their smiling faces confused me and made me mad. They didn't have a problem...I did! I was not happy. How could they be smiling when my world was falling apart?

Friends, just in well-meaning conversation would share with me about their children going to college and how bad they were going to miss their son or daughter. They would continue telling me how they didn't know how they were going to make it without their child. Sometimes I would be dumb-founded at the insensitive comments I would hear. However, how could these dear friends measure my loss and know my pain? Actually, they couldn't. I had to learn to release that hurt and let it go. I gave it to God...because it was too big for me to handle.

I also continued reading my Bible, hoping God would give me an answer. Finally, as I tuned my heart to listen to God, I remember these words ringing emphatically in my thoughts *I am a good God.*

I started to truly understand in my heart that we cannot measure His goodness based upon whether good things or bad things happen to us as Christians or even-non Christians, good people or bad people. *I was learning to see God as good because of who He is and not because of what He does or provides.* His goodness is not based upon whether good things or bad things happen. His goodness results in His promise to be with you and me in the good times and in the bad times; "I will never leave you, nor forsake you" (Deuteronomy 31:6).

We live in this world affected and stained by sin, death and destruction. Many times our physical bodies, our situations and circumstances may be altered or succumb to the unrelenting attributes of sin in this life. However, the good news is Jesus Christ has conquered over sin, death, hell and the grave (1 Corinthians 15:55-57). As Christians, we have a hope and a promise beyond this world. I had to rely on the lesson about God being a good God to get through the physical separation with Christopher.

My thought was if God is good, Christopher would not have died.

Honestly, I grew up with a tainted philosophy of my relationship with God. I thought because I was a Christian, and grew up in a Christian home and loved God at an early age, He would take care of me and not let anything bad happen. He would supply my every need. I was thinking of God more as a "genie in a bottle" who would grant my every wish rather than a loving Father helping me to grow and mature and become more like Him, even in adversity.

I woke up and found out God's goodness is based upon the promise that when we are discouraged or go through tragedies and tough times He will be with us. He said,

> *I have told you these things, so that in Me you may have [perfect] peace and confidence. In the world you have tribulation and trials and distress and frustration; but be of good cheer [take courage; be confident, certain, undaunted]! For I have overcome the world. [I have deprived it of power to harm you and have conquered it for you* (John 16:32-33) AMP.

I cannot begin to tell you how liberating that revelation of the Word of God was to me. God was indeed good and had not let me down.

He was and always will be good, not based upon what happens to us, but because of who He is and what He is doing in and through you and me. I was beginning to understand that God allows our lives to be sprinkled with blessings and trials for His divine appointment and purpose for our lives. This understanding allows me to realize that we can *Party In The Pit*.

Survival Tip: **Remember that God is good...*even in the pit.***

Verse: **Psalm 107:1**
O give thanks unto the LORD, for he is good: for his mercy endureth forever

Divine Appointments – *by Joy Ware Miller, 2006*

From one sad situation
to another…right before your eyes.

A mess - confusion - heartache - loss,
seems to be on the rise.

You question God - you feel alone…
where could He possibly be?

Miracles come - prayers are answered…
but not always the way I want for me.

At times, it seems - unclear - unfair…
I'm almost lost in the fray.

And yet…that still small voice
so gently calls… "I am the truth, I am the way."

All would be lost if I did not remember…
God's promises are true.

This earth is temporary - training ground,
and yes…we will go through.

Tough Times - hard and tragic loss…
somewhat like Jesus…on the cross.

He knows our pain, He sees the tears -
and with joy, He's conquered death, hell and ALL our fears.

The promise of Heaven
answers all our disappointments…

As we travel through life each and every day…
Trusting His divine appointments!

CHAPTER TWO

understanding My Purpose

Purpose ~ courageous men and women

Life is a series of experiences, each one of which makes us bigger, even though it is hard to realize this. For the world was built to develop character, and we must learn that the setbacks and griefs which we endure help us in our marching onward.

Henry Ford (1863-1947)

~ ~ ~ ~ ~

Our society is consumed with the have-it-your-way, because-you-are-worth-it and you only-live-once attitudes. Webster's Online Dictionary defines self-centered as "independent of outside force or influence; self-sufficient or concerned solely with one's own desire, needs or interest." Many people in our society are self-sufficient and concerned only about themselves. They do not recognize God as the Creator and accept (or believe) that He has a divine purpose for each of us. The *American Dream* portrays the idea that it's all about me, my fast track, my house on the hill with a three-car garage, my 2.5 kids, my elaborate vacations every year and my reaching retirement before sixty-five only to travel and enjoy recreational time as the purpose for living. Most of us strive to be happy, content and successful. If we have the good fortune to achieve the *American Dream,* then society says we have definitely *made it.* We are a success. But, what do we really have? We have a mortgage, bills, and demanding responsibilities. Now understand there is absolutely nothing wrong with attaining the *American Dream.* However, do we strive with the same effort to accomplish *God's Dream* and to please Him? What about making God happy and finding contentment in Him? Finding our purpose in Christ allows us to see how successful we can be sharing His Gospel and following His blueprint for our lives.

Which dream has our heart? Our very existence is all about Him. The only things that we can take with us throughout eternity are our family members and friends. What we do for God will outlast any part of the *American Dream.* Funny how we are taught to think life

revolves around us, and what we acquire here on earth. The
scripture in Colossians reveals our purpose:

> *He is the image of the invisible God, the first born*
> *over all creation. For by Him all things were*
> *created; things in heaven and on earth, visible and*
> *invisible, whether thrones or power or rulers or*
> *authorities; all things were created by Him and for*
> *Him. He is before all things, and in Him all things*
> *hold together* (Colossians 1:15-17).

God is always working on His purposes in and through our lives.

Courageous Men and Women Who Found Their Purpose
"Partying In The Pit"

I am sure the day started out normally for Meshach, Shadrach and
Abednego; however these three young Hebrew men facing the
journey of a lifetime, were destined for a purpose. During the reign
of King Nebuchadnezzar, these young men refused to denounce their
true and living God. They would not bow to King Nebuchadnezzar
as their higher authority. They were taking a stand for God. So I am
pretty sure they were astonished and disappointed when they were

arrested for civil disobedience and thrown into a fiery furnace. The furnace was extremely hot and heated seven times hotter than usual. Even the guards outside the furnace were burned and died as a result of the heat: *The king's command was so urgent and the furnace so hot that the flames of the fire killed the soldiers who took up Shadrach, Meshach and Abednego* (Daniel 3:22).

You know these three Hebrew men experienced and sensed God's divine appointment because while in the fire the fourth man showed up and old King Nebuchadnezzar stated, "He looks like the Son of God" (Daniel 3:25). The presence of God was with them during their fiery trial as they were *Partying in the Pit* and standing in faith. These young men did not burn or even smell like smoke! God had a great plan and purpose for Meshach, Shadrach and Abednego in leadership and authority.

What was God doing? What is God doing in your life?

Paul and Silas were mighty men of God and purpose. They were traveling together doing good, preaching the Gospel and healing the sick and setting the oppressed free in the name of Jesus. Consequently, their journey would be full of persecution and would lead them to prison because of their love and service to the Lord. It was midnight, again, and you can imagine they were somewhat disappointed to be chained and still in prison, *About midnight Paul and Silas were praying and singing hymns to God, and the other prisoners were listening to them* (Acts 16:25).

However, these two men of faith chose in the midst of disappointment and sorrow, in their midnight hour, to sing and see God's mighty power move! God had a great plan and purpose for Paul and Silas and used them mightily for His glory!

What was God doing? What is God doing in your life?

Moses was adopted into royalty, living in the King's palace experiencing the *good life*. His purpose at that time was to have others serve him. Moses was being groomed for Egyptian royal leadership and authority. Needless-to-say, he was somewhat disappointed and confused when his true identity was revealed. Moses ended up in the desert, far away from the palace and was no longer being served, but learning how to serve. Little did he know, he would eventually be leading the Hebrews out of bondage and would be in authority over at least twelve Hebrew tribes. God had a great plan and purpose for Moses as a deliverer of His people. *So now, go. I am sending you to Pharaoh to bring my people the Israelites out of Egypt* (Exodus 3:10).

What was God doing? What is God doing in your life?

Prime Minister Daniel was from the Hebrew Court and taken as a prisoner into Babylonian captivity. Daniel could have thought, when in Babylon, do as the Babylonians do and worship idols. However, even as a prisoner, Daniel knew his purpose and would not compromise his faith: *But Daniel resolved not to defile himself with the royal food and wine, and he asked the chief official for*

permission not to defile himself this way (Daniel 1:8).

Daniel refused to be silent. He would not quit praying to his God,
Jehovah. No doubt, he was somewhat disappointed to find out that
his integrity and commitment to keep praying to God would land
him in the lions' den. God had a great plan and purpose for Daniel,
and He shut the mouths of the lions and Daniel's accusers.

> *When he came near the den, he called to Daniel in*
> *an anguished voice, "Daniel, servant of the living*
> *God, has your God, whom you serve continually,*
> *been able to rescue you from the lions?" Daniel*
> *answered, "O king, live forever! My God sent his*
> *angel and he shut the mouths of the lions. They have*
> *not hurt me, because I was found innocent in his*
> *sight. Nor have I ever done any wrong before you, O*
> *king." The king was overjoyed and gave orders to lift*
> *Daniel out of the den. And when Daniel was lifted*
> *from the den, no wound was found on him, because he*
> *had trusted in his God. At the king's command, the*
> *men who had falsely accused Daniel were brought in*
> *and thrown into the lions' den, along with their wives*

and children. And before they reached the floor of
the den, the lions overpowered them and crushed all
their bones (Daniel 6:20-24).

What was God doing? What is God doing in your life?

Joseph believed he had somewhat of an idea about his purpose

and destiny at a young age through several dreams. He dreamed that

his brothers would one day bow to him and that he would become a

man of influence and greatness.

> *When he told his father as well as his brothers, his*
> *father rebuked him and said, 'What is this dream you*
> *had? Will your mother and I and your brothers*
> *actually come and bow down to the ground before*
> *you?'* (Genesis 37:10).

Why would Joseph be mistreated by his brothers, sold into

slavery and endure many long years of hopelessness? It just does

not seem fair. Favored by his father, but rejected by his brothers, I

am sure he was disappointed with his life and what God was

allowing to happen. Moreover, Joseph was *growing through what he was going through* and becoming who God wanted him to be.

Joseph kept hoping in God and did not give up. Joseph's ability to dream and his God-given gift to interpret dreams catapulted him from the prison to the palace as second in command to Pharaoh. God had a great plan and purpose for Joseph. His brothers did bow to him and he did become a man of influence and greatness to save the nation of Israel.

What was God doing? What is God doing in your life?

Esther was a young Jewish girl with beauty and charm, minding her own business. God had plans for Esther and would use her to save the Jewish nation. Esther was under pressure to speak to the king for her people and her decision put her life in jeopardy and would change the course of history. With such great responsibility came great ability through God…because she had been born for such a time as this (Esther 4:14).

What was God doing? What is God doing in your life?

Jesus, God's son, knew no sin. He did nothing wrong and owed absolutely nothing. He was perfect, sitting at the right hand of His Father, God. I'm sure it was not an easy choice to give up His throne and come to earth as a baby, grow as a man and experience the full array of humanity and have it sit on his shoulder: *For to us a child is born, to us a son is given, and the government will be on his shoulders. And he will be called Wonderful Counselor, Mighty God, Everlasting Father, Prince of Peace* (Isaiah 9:6).

Jesus knew His purpose and *willingly* endured the cross, the agony, sadness, separation, heartache, sin and torture. Why? The answer is He did so for you and for me. *For God so loved the world that He gave His only begotten son, that whosoever believeth on Him should not perish but have everlasting life: for God sent not His son to condemn the world but that the world might be saved through Him* (John 3:16-17).

What was God doing? What is God doing in your life?

Jesus is our example. He has felt and tasted every heartache, disappointment and tragedy known to mankind. He continues to pave the way as *The Way*. We do not ever have to believe the lies of the enemy that God doesn't care, or that He is not here for us. When we see what God is doing and quit looking at our circumstances, God is able to give us vision, which takes us past our limited sight.

God is in the business of creating character, trust, faith, strength, fortitude, obedience, love and joy. He is creating us to be *Christ-like*. He is forming destiny, creating history and bringing about deliverance from sin unto Himself and salvation. *I have found that He is more concerned about our character than our comfort, our spiritual than material "wants", obedience than sacrifice, and eternity than the here and now.* Trusting Him with what we cannot see rather than what we can see is our constant faith journey.

God wants to create, magnify and bring about beauty that reflects Himself supernaturally out of the chaos, struggles, pressures, fire and even tragedies that we face. God wants to use our lives to bring Himself glory.

> *Therefore, since we have been justified through faith, we have peace with God through our Lord Jesus Christ, through whom we have gained access by faith into this grace in which we now stand. And we boast in the hope of the glory of God. Not only so, but we also glory in our sufferings, because we know that suffering produces perseverance; perseverance, character; and character, hope. And hope does not put us to shame, because God's love has been poured out into our hearts through the Holy Spirit, who has been given to us* (Romans 5:1-5).

Just like Christian in John Bunyan's allegory *Pilgrim's Progress,* we grow through each experience we go through in life. The pearl, once a small bit of sand, becomes beautiful through agitation. Metal purified through fire becomes perfect through intense heat. We become who God intends for us to be, while on the journey, keeping Heaven in view. Character is built, tenacity found, and strength increased with every decision not to give up and quit. He wants us to become the *Fragrance of Christ* and establish Godliness, faith, trust, confidence and love in our lives and in the lives of those around us. He wants us to gain His perspective as we learn to *Party in the Pit*.

Survival Tips: **My purpose is to please the Father and give Him glory...*even in the Pit.***

Verse: **Colossians 1:16 (AMP)**

> *For it was in Him that all things were created, in heaven and on earth, things seen and things unseen, whether thrones, dominions, rulers, or authorities; all things were created and exist through Him [by His service, intervention] and in and for Him.*

The Fragrance of Christ – *by Joy Ware Miller, 2003*

I think about His fragrance
His light and love for you.
So much He has in store
each day, and all year through.

His presence goes before us
directing all the way.
His protection completely keeps us
in a perverse and wicked day.

Without Him, I would lose my mind
with doubt and fear and dread.
But with Him, I'll go all the way
He's the lifter of my head.

No longer do I mope and grope
and grasp for greener grass.
The direction God's got me going
I'm growing…and that's the task.
His presence fills our lives with
His fragrance from above.
Can you sense it?
Can you tell it?
It's yours too
From God, with love.

CHAPTER THREE

In The Pit and Gaining God's Perspective

Perspective ~ His thoughts versus our thoughts

The best we can hope for in this life is a knothole peek at the shining realities ahead. Yet a glimpse is enough. It's enough to convince our hearts that whatever sufferings and sorrows currently assail us aren't worthy of comparison to that which waits over the horizon.

Joni Eareckson Tada

~ ~ ~ ~ ~

The definition of *perspective* is to see clearly or to look. It may be hard to believe, but God is working in our lives on a daily basis. I not only see this now with our separation with Christopher, but in every aspect of my life: at work, with my neighbors or even at church and definitely at home with my family. However, we are often unaware of His handiwork because we are trying to see life from our own perspective. This letter written by a college student to her parents helps us understand the importance of perspective:

Dear Mom and Dad,

I was just writing home to let you know that everything is well...well at least as well as it can be expected after I totaled the car.

No need to worry though, Lenny has been wonderful. He's the man who rescued me just before the car exploded. Lenny has been taking excellent care of me and this arrangement has worked out great since Lenny is legally blind, homeless and has not found a job or a place to stay since getting out of prison two months ago!

Lenny and I have fallen so madly in love, I will be dropping out of school right before the baby is due. I should be able to deliver naturally even with both legs still in traction.

Our faith is strong and will carry us through even when my insurance runs out at the end of this month.

Love you dearly, Your Daughter and new Son-in-law!

P.S. I did not have an accident, there is no Lenny, I am not pregnant, my insurance is fine and I'm not dropping out of school. <u>However, I just wanted you to be able to put my D in Chemistry in proper PERSPECTIVE.</u>

Proper perspective puts us on the same page as God. His perspective encourages us to live in a dimension of faith, hope and courage.

> *For my thoughts are not your thoughts, neither are your ways my ways, declares the LORD. As the heavens are higher than the earth, so are my ways higher than your ways and my thoughts than your thoughts* (Isaiah 55:8-9).

So many of us spend so much of our waking hours trying to be happy and comfortable, avoiding pain of any kind on every level. Everyone would like to avoid conflict and struggles. Who wouldn't? However, it seems inevitable to run from the struggles, and quite frankly the struggles produce some of the most exquisite beauty from the butterfly to the pearl. It all comes back to perspective. We can find many examples of beauty produced through endless struggles, un-natural pressures and intense fire just like our courageous men and women who found perspective in the pit. The butterfly's exquisite detail, and markings along with its ability to fly result from struggling within the cocoon. If the caterpillar quits struggling too soon, it will never reach its beautiful potential and ability to fly. The pearl becomes priceless through constant agitation. The longer the agitation lasts, the bigger the pearl will become! A diamond is nothing more than a lump of coal, polished with a lot of pressure. The wealth of the diamond is there all along but it takes time and pressure to expose the hidden sparkle.

Purifying metal is one of my favorite examples of how gold and silver are only useful once the imperfections are gone. Sounds simple enough; however, it is the excruciating heat of the fire that prepares the precious metal. The metal is so hot that it becomes liquid and the impurities float to the top becoming visible and then discarded.

God allows the struggles, agitation, pressure and fires of life to stretch and mold us into His image. The *fiery trials* have a way of purifying our character and attitudes, creating beauty from a lump of coal. We would not easily learn how to fly and spread our wings, or become polished and realize our wealth of potential and gain that hidden sparkle, if we avoided the pits of life. God's thoughts and plans are so different from ours. Instead of asking "why me?" let's start asking "what do you want to do through and in me?"

His Thoughts versus Our Thoughts!

God's thoughts are not our thoughts, but they should be. God's thoughts include living and acting on faith regarding what is not seen, even when it seems impossible to be true. Man lives by what he sees and understands is possible. God plans for eternity and man plans for time. We hunker down and become intimate with the world. We start to see everything based upon time and not God's view of eternity. Actually, we have all the time in the world, because God is not limited to time. God's ways are supernatural, and man's way is natural. Confidence in science and what we can touch and see, is easier to explain because of man's reasoning. It is only natural we think…and therein is the problem. God's ways are unlimited, and man's way is limited. We can go or think only so far in advance and then we reach our limit. Where we stop…is actually, where God can begin.

Our God rejoices while in persecution and trouble, which is extremely difficult to grasp because man fights back and resents and wants revenge. Our God labors and gives to others, while man labors for self and does not want to share. As we realize and focus on God's thoughts and become more like Him, His thoughts and ways will become a part of us. We will not only see what God is seeing, but also understand what He is doing.

Survival Tip: My perspective should be viewed through God's eyes…*even in the pit.*

Verse: **Isaiah 55:8-9**
For my thoughts are not your thoughts, neither are your ways my ways, declares the LORD. As the heavens are higher than the earth, so are my ways higher than your ways and my thoughts than your thoughts.

His PERSPECTIVE – by Joy Ware Miller, 2012

Perspective helps me clear the view
to see God's way is true.
His ways are so much higher,
His thoughts toward me and you.

Sometimes I feel so blocked
by my thoughts and what's around.
God's Word however, is the key
that wipes away my frown.

His Word, His Thoughts of hope and joy
and what He sees ahead.
Life everlasting, His love so real
just like the Bible said.

I want to see like Jesus
Finding strength within the weak,
looking into darkness to
find the silver streak.

His Perspective - continued

Seeing what He sees first
is the lesson I strive to impart.
Each day gives me opportunity
to have His vision and His heart.

CHAPTER FOUR

It's All Or Nothing In The Pit

Promise ~ Hope is everything

Without Christ there is no hope.
Charles Spurgeon (1834-1892)

~ ~ ~ ~ ~

Hope is what will lead you down a dark hall anticipating the light at the end. Hope is what will cause you to exercise to get into that smaller swimsuit regardless of what the mirror says. Hope is what allows a mother to endure labor in order to hold her newborn baby. The hope of Heaven is what will sustain us in our darkest hour because it brings promise in our adversity.

Heaven is the answer to anything lost or broken. Heaven does not just mend; it renews and restores. Nothing missing, nothing broken. *Christ offers us eternal hope to endure our temporary pain.* Chapter four is my favorite chapter because God's promise offers us hope even in the Pit. The promise of God's Word gives us comfort, strength, wisdom and deliverance through tough times here on earth in the midst of despair and difficulty. This was the liberating moment for me. I thought I would never smile or laugh again. My heart seemed too heavy to laugh and when I smiled, I felt fake.

Then came a glimmer of hope. I realized the price Jesus paid for my salvation and my freedom from death. Jesus paid for my happiness in Heaven and my ability through Him to endure and overcome disappointment and heartache on earth. As Christians, we really have a win – win scenario. We win when we live and we win when our bodies die. That's called eternity. How do you want to spend yours? The heartache you are facing; the sadness you feel; the disease that has robbed; the disability, whether physical or emotional that you face daily, will end. We will not be separated from our loved ones again. All of the things we are *going through* here will one day be over...when we are there. The crying will stop and the rejoicing will begin.

And God shall wipe away all tears from their eyes;
and there shall be no more death, neither sorrow, nor
crying, neither shall there be any more pain: for the
former things are passed away" (Revelation 21:4).

Heaven answers, reconciles, redeems, renews, and rewards all of those *injustices* we felt were inflicted upon us and other Christians during this life on earth. We can know this for sure because of the promise of Christ and His resurrection power to *make all things new.*

And he that sat upon the throne said, Behold, I make
all things new. And he said unto me, Write: for these
words are true and faithful" (Revelation 21:5).

Christ died, to give us life. That resurrection power is the life-blood of our faith and hope, which strengthens us to live life in light of eternity. Every day holds opportunities for God to use us for His purpose. Through our attitudes, actions and reactions, God is able to use us for His *Purpose* as we gain His *Perspective* and remember to hold onto His *Promises.*

Hebrews chapter eleven is well known as *The Faith* chapter. This chapter is full of accounts of men and woman of faith who stood the test, received immediate miraculous outcomes and testified of God's awesome power.

This chapter also lists men and woman of faith who stood the test, and *did not* receive immediate miraculous outcomes. The people who did not receive immediate miraculous outcomes are my favorite group of people, because I relate to them well. They continued in faith with hope of God's promise without seeing or receiving anything for their declaration, and sometimes for their sacrifice of faith this side of Heaven. I have found it is easy to witness to God's goodness when everything is going your way…but much more of a challenge when your circumstances and situations turn out unexpectedly and contrary to your hopes, plans and dreams.

What type of people would we be if we got everything we wanted, the way we wanted, when we wanted it? SPOILED! Just like a child who gets their way all of the time. Life brings challenges to challenge our faith and help us grow. God gives us His Word to use as a weapon to build our faith and win the victory.

This chapter in Hebrews will help you focus when you are in the Pit. Hebrews chapter eleven tells us that faith is being sure of what we hope for and certain of what we do not see. I challenge you to read the entire chapter...and find yourself in the Hall of Faith. You will find courage, strength, hope and fortitude within this chapter in the Bible. You will read about families and individuals loving God enough to pick up and leave their homes and go to unknown places; encounter couples who long for a child and endure a lifelong wait; realize the agony of surrendering your son...and having him given back to you.

Read thoroughly through this chapter and take a glimpse of normal men and women who did not necessarily obtain their promise, but died having hope. Their hope was not in receiving something material, which some did receive and some did not, but their hope and their trust was in God.

In this chapter, many conquered kingdoms, administered justice, and obtained what was promised. Others fought battles, sacrificed their lives, and gave up everything as they were mistreated and humiliated knowing their reward was eternal. The people in this chapter reveal remarkable character, belief and trust in God. They are not thinking that God owes them something, but rather they are offering their life as service to Him. They share a humble and reverent spirit, which fuels their hope in Christ.

Realizing Truth In The Pit

The hardest disappointment for me was expecting God to honor His Word the way I anticipated. That is when I would drop my hope and find myself embracing discouragement. "You didn't do it my way, God...so I'm mad at you". I failed to remember God is Sovereign and my expectations and His truth did not always match. Like the folks in Hebrews 11, I had to learn to humble myself and respect God in His Sovereignty, which in turn, continued to give me hope.

With every birthday, holiday and special moment I no longer share with Christopher here on earth, I still know God's promises are true. Let me be very clear about the Word of God. God's Word is unquestionable and true all of the time. Moreover, God is not obligated to execute His plan my way. He is bound by His Word and can exercise His Sovereignty in any way, at any time, all of the time. Once again, we must relinquish and surrender our will daily to God's purpose, perspective and promise regarding our lives as we continue to hope in Him.

Survival Tips: **God never breaks a promise, and is not bound by time. We can live life in light of eternity! (even in the pit)**

Verse: **Psalm 145:13**

Your kingdom is an everlasting kingdom, and your dominion endures through all generations. The LORD is trustworthy in all he promises and faithful in all he does.

Accounted Unto Righteousness – by Joy Ware Miller, 2011

For those who endured and kept their faith,
It is accounted as unto righteousness.

For those who persevered and kept believing,
It is accounted as unto righteousness.

For those who lived through an abusive relationship trusting God to
deliver them,
It is accounted as unto righteousness.

For those who served the Lord and were wrongly mistreated,
It is accounted as unto righteousness.

For those who prayed and are still patiently waiting for an answer,
It is accounted as unto righteousness.

For those who have everything going wrong, but continue to love,
serve and hope in the Lord,
It is accounted as unto righteousness.

Eternity will prove time was only momentary for the righteous.

CHAPTER FIVE

Becoming A Lean Mean Pit Party Machine

Finally, it's time to "Party In The Pit"

We all know people who have been made much meaner, more irritable, and more intolerable to live with by suffering: it is not right to say that all suffering perfects. It only perfects one type of person...the one who accepts the call of God in Christ Jesus.
Oswald Chambers (1874-1917)

~ ~ ~ ~ ~

Do you remember the *"get out of jail free card"* in the popular board game *Monopoly*? Everyone always wanted to have that card for reassurance that if something happened, if plans changed, they would be able to once-again-gain their freedom. What can we use in real life when *things* don't turn out the way we dreamed or planned? We feel captive, bound, held prisoner not necessarily behind real bars, but in our thoughts, emotions and circumstances. We need a free *get out of the pit card*.

If there were such a card, the word on it would be S.U.R.R.E.N.D.E.R. Surrender means to relinquish, give up, give over to, and yield to the power, control, or possession of another. Paul stated:

> *Do you not know that your body is the temple (the very sanctuary) of the Holy Spirit Who lives within you, Whom you have received [as a Gift] from God? You are not your own, You were bought with a price [purchased with a preciousness and paid for, made His own]. So then, honor God and bring glory to Him in your body* (1 Corinthians 6:19-20 AMP).

I found that when I truly surrendered everything-- my past, present and future over to the Lord-- I no longer had any rights to fuss, complain or disagree with the *purpose* God had designed for me. I relinquished my will for His. I gave up my desires and gave them over to Him. I yielded power and control to God. That included my finances, career, spouse, children, expectations and even timing. That included Christopher and his unexpected departure from earth and anticipated arrival in Heaven. I had to relinquish my will, give up my dreams, and yield to His power and control as I began to see everything through God's *perspective*. I had to believe Proverbs 3:5: *Trust in the Lord with all your heart and lean not to your own understanding, but in all your ways acknowledge Him and He shall direct your path.*

We can also see TRUST as an acronym **T**otal **R**eliance **U**nder **S**tressful **T**imes! Through surrendering, I am saying "yes" to Christ and "no" to self. Through surrendering, I become a pliable servant for Christ.

Here is the important key. As we surrender to God's will, our will becomes one with His. It's not His way or my way...it is *The* way. Through surrendering, we become one in *purpose*. I want what God wants and God wants what I want. Instead of the *American Dream* we spoke of earlier, we begin to realize and discover *God's Dream* that was designed for us before we were born. *"For I know the plans I have for you,"* declares the LORD, *"plans to prosper you and not to harm you, plans to give you hope and a future"* (Jeremiah 29:11).

Do you love Jesus more...to surrender everything to Him? Will you surrender your heart? Your disappointments? Your questions? Your will? Are you willing to surrender your past, present and future?

STOP. Right now. Do not read any further until you settle this question...and the call from Christ for you to surrender to Him because He loves you. I invite you right now to ask Jesus Christ into your heart as Savior and Lord or renew your relationship right now.

> *For God so loved the world that he gave his one and only Son, that whoever believes in him shall not perish but have eternal life. For God did not send his Son into the world to condemn the world, but to save the world through him* (John 3:16-17).

Jesus died that you might have life. However, He gives us the choice to accept His free gift of salvation. My prayer is that you open your heart and ask Jesus into your life. That does not mean everything will be instantly wonderful. It does mean God will be with you in the good times and the difficult times. It also means you are on your way to Heaven. Make that declaration of your new life in Christ based upon Romans 10:9 (AMP).

> *Because if you acknowledge and confess with your lips that Jesus is Lord and in your heart believe (adhere to, trust in, and rely on the truth) that God raised Him from the dead, you will be saved.*

Amen! If you said "yes," all of Heaven is rejoicing and so am I. Congratulations! Send me an email…and share your story! We can't wait to rejoice with you! Now comes the part of growing stronger in the Word of God. It is the Word of God, the knowledge of the truth and the application of that truth that prepares us with the correct tools to be victorious and see God's Word manifest in our lives.

As Christians, we are daily thrust into various arenas whether home, work or other activities, both pleasant and at times tragic, that allow us to recognize whether we have really surrendered everything to the Lord. You may wonder like me, "Is God playing games?" The answer is always "No." *God is allowing and orchestrating corporate and individual events in our lives to groom us for eternity.* I believe God is more concerned about our inward self than our circumstances around us.

He wants us to be prepared and to help others to prepare for eternity, by knowing Him as Savior and Lord. We tend to get *off track* and blinded to why we were created. We need to focus on sharing the salvation message of Jesus Christ. Not only should we be sharing, but we should be living our testimony every day in front of others and wanting to take as many friends, relatives, neighbors, co-workers, and acquaintances as possible with us to Heaven.

Believe me; others will take notice when you decide to *Party In The Pit* while you are living through adversity. They will recognize your faith, admire your strength and have to acknowledge your God. In our weaknesses, He is made strong. Our goal is to live above our circumstances in the face of adversity and continue to give God glory!

But we have this treasure in jars of clay to show that
this all-surpassing power is from God and not from
us. We are hard pressed on every side, but not
crushed; perplexed, but not in despair; persecuted,
but not abandoned; struck down, but not destroyed.
We always carry around in our body the death of
Jesus, so that the life of Jesus may also be revealed in
our body. For we who are alive are always being
given over to death for Jesus' sake, so that his life
may also be revealed in our mortal body. So then,
death is at work in us, but life is at work in you
(2 Cor. 4:7-12).

Are you ready to live a victorious life even in the midst of adversity? Are you ready to relinquish your will, your dreams and see what God has planned? Are you ready to quit asking why and start asking what is the lesson and what should I do next? Are you ready to stop looking at the world's system and cling to God's *perspective* through His Word? Are you ready to give up your disappointment for His appointment?

Are you ready to RSVP and choose to *Party In The Pit*?

Survival Tip: **I will choose to surrender and "Party Even In The Pit"**

Verse: **Philippians 3:13-14**

...But one thing I do: Forgetting what is behind and straining toward what is ahead, I press on toward the goal to win the prize for which God has called me heavenward in Christ Jesus.

Surrender The Sorrow – Joy Ware Miller, 2005

The pain of separation
no one ever is prepared.

All the hopes and dreams and
joys so intimately shared.

Making plans for the future
watching them grow up. . .

Never thinking or even dreaming
that such tragedy would fill your cup!

Many years, or only a few together,
making memories in your heart.

Trinkets - pictures - trophies
now ...packed all in a cart.

Knowing each day brings its pain
and joy is offered too -

Gaining strength and comfort from above
is what we each must do.

I am finding healing will not come in avoiding tomorrow -
but hope is held each brand new day,
as you willingly "*Surrender The Sorrow*!"

Believers Pit Manual
and
Special Note From Joy

31 Daily Confessions…While In The Pit
Speak Each Confession Out Loud
Don't Just Think It…Speak It!

Definition of "Pitology" – *the study of living in the pit and how to*

find purpose, perspective and promise that preps you to party in the

pit and live in victory!

* _Day 1:_ I have been saved through Grace…it is a gift from God because I have purpose.

Ephesians 2:8

For it is by grace you have been saved, through faith—and this is not from yourselves, it is the gift of God.

* _Day 2:_ I see my life through God's vision…and His perspective only.

Isaiah 55:8-9

For my thoughts are not your thoughts, neither are your ways my ways, declares the Lord. As the heavens are higher than the earth, so are my ways higher than your ways and my thoughts than your thoughts.

* _Day 3:_ I accept all of God's promises as truth...eternity will reveal my complete victory.

2 Corinthians 1:20

For no matter how many promises God has made, they are Yes in Christ. And so through him the Amen is spoken by us to the glory of God.

* _Day 4:_ I believe God's Word, even when I don't see...that is called faith.

Hebrews 11:1

Now faith is confidence in what we hope for and assurance about what we do not see.

* _Day 5:_ Courage is me standing strong...in the face of fear (this calls for a growl).

Joshua 1:9

Have I not commanded you? Be strong and courageous. Do not be afraid; do not be discouraged, for the Lord your God will be with you wherever you go.

* _Day 6:_ I know that God is good...regardless of what my situation looks like.

Psalm 106:1

Praise the Lord. Give thanks to the Lord, for he is good; his love endures forever.

* _Day 7:_ I believe the best is yet to come…because He is faithful who promised.

Hebrews 10:23

Let us hold unswervingly to the hope we profess, for he who promised is faithful.

* _Day 8:_ I will pray…and only expect God's answer, even if it's not what I wanted.

Matthew 6:9-10

This, then, is how you should pray: Our Father in Heaven, hallowed be your name,
your kingdom come, your will be done, on earth as it is in Heaven.

* _Day 9:_ I will look for opportunities to bless others…who have been hurt.

2 Corinthians 1:3-4

Praise be to the God and Father of our Lord Jesus Christ, the Father of compassion and the God of all comfort, who comforts us in all our troubles, so that we can comfort those in any trouble with the comfort we ourselves receive from God.

* _Day 10:_ I realize money isn't everything…God supplies my every need.

Matthew 6:33

But seek first his kingdom and his righteousness, and all these things will be given to you as well.

* _Day 11:_ I will surrender to God's will…it's His way and not mine.

Psalm 40:8

I desire to do your will, my God; your law is within my heart.

* _Day 12:_ I will remember to be humble…because pride will lead me to fall.

Proverbs 16:18

Pride goes before destruction, a haughty spirit before a fall.

* _Day 13:_ Commitment is when I stay true…to the promises I have made.

Hebrews 10:22

Let us draw near to God with a sincere heart and with the full assurance that faith brings, having our hearts sprinkled to cleanse us from a guilty conscience and having our bodies washed with pure water.

* _Day 14:_ Trust is holding on…but better yet God is holding me.

Proverbs 3:5-6

Trust in the LORD with all your heart and lean not on your own understanding; in all your ways submit to him, and he will make your paths straight.

* _Day 15:_ I will lean into the difficulty…because God is helping me grow through what I go through.

2 Corinthians 4:7-9

But we have this treasure in jars of clay to show that this all-surpassing power is from God and not from us. We are hard pressed on every side, but not crushed; perplexed, but not in despair; persecuted, but not abandoned; struck down, but not destroyed.

* _Day 16:_ I trust God…He is turning my tragedy into His triumph.

1 Peter 5:8-11

Be alert and of sober mind. Your enemy the devil prowls around like a roaring lion looking for someone to devour. Resist him, standing firm in the faith, because you know that the family of believers throughout the world is undergoing the same kind of sufferings.

And the God of all grace, who called you to his eternal glory in Christ, after you have suffered a little while, will himself restore you and make you strong, firm and steadfast. To him be the power forever and ever. Amen.

* _Day 17:_ I see life way past death…because of Christ we have the final victory.

1 Corinthians 15:55

Where, O death, is your victory? Where, O death, is your sting?

* _Day 18:_ I always win in spite of failure…because I will not quit.

Philippians 3:4

I press on toward the goal to win the prize for which God has called me heavenward in Christ Jesus.

* _Day 19:_ My heart is healing even when I hurt…because Christ is with me, He gives me hope.

1 Peter 1:3

Praise be to the God and Father of our Lord Jesus Christ! In his great mercy he has given us new birth into a living hope through the resurrection of Jesus Christ from the dead.

* _Day 20:_ I'm moving past procrastination to motivation…that's my battle cry.

Proverbs 6:6

Go to the ant, you sluggard; consider its ways and be wise!

* _Day 21:_ I'm finding health in sickness…because it's offered in God's Word.

Isaiah 53:5

But he was pierced for our transgressions, he was crushed for our iniquities; the punishment that brought us peace was on him, and by his wounds we are healed.

* _Day 22:_ I'm looking at the ups through the downs...and gaining God's perspective.

Psalm 53:5

In the morning, LORD, you hear my voice; in the morning I lay my requests before you and wait expectantly.

* _Day 23:_ I'm pursuing joy in the midst of heartache...because there is joy in the morning.

Psalm 30:5

For his anger lasts only a moment, but his favor lasts a lifetime; weeping may stay for the night, but rejoicing comes in the morning.

* _Day 24:_ I'm finding sanity in craziness, because I must...the Word renews my mind.

Romans 12:2

Do not conform to the pattern of this world, but be transformed by the renewing of your mind. Then you will be able to test and approve what God's will is—his good, pleasing and perfect will.

* _Day 25:_ I believe the truth is no lie...God never lies.

John 17:17

Sanctify them by the truth; your word is truth.

* _Day 26:_ I will smile in sorrow…because it is possible.

Mark 10:27

Jesus looked at them and said, With man this is impossible, but not with God; all things are possible with God.

* _Day 27:_ I'm saved…I don't want to go back.

Romans 10:9

If you declare with your mouth, "Jesus is Lord," and believe in your heart that God raised him from the dead, you will be saved.

* _Day 28:_ I seek order out of chaos…and there is peace.

Romans 15:13

May the God of hope fill you with all joy and peace as you trust in him, so that you may overflow with hope by the power of the Holy Spirit.

* _Day 29:_ I recognize delight in devastation…because I have God's discernment.

Psalm 119:125

I am your servant; give me discernment that I may understand your statutes.

* _Day 30:_ I realize joy in pain…because I am being formed in His precious image.

2 Corinthians 3:18

And we all, who with unveiled faces contemplate the Lord's glory, are being transformed into his image with ever-increasing glory, which comes from the Lord, who is the Spirit.

* _Day 31:_ I strive for progress in setbacks…because I know He holds my future.

Jeremiah 29:11

For I know the plans I have for you, declares the Lord, plans to prosper you and not to harm you, plans to give you hope and a future.

* Special Note From Joy:

My heart's cry for us all…is that we will always be diligent to seek God, run to Him and delicately find the hope and healing power of the treasure and triumph over the tragedy and trash that we may endure while in the pit, knowing There's a Party In The Pit…and You Are Invited! RSVP… I will see you there!

ABOUT THE AUTHOR

Christian women's speaker, author, inspirational coach, voice actor, President, iJoy Inspirations, Founder, Parents On Call, Joy Ware Miller has a powerful message of hope. A down-to-earth, dynamic and authentic friend, her message is uplifting and her testimony moving as she helps women work through their disappointment and hopeless feelings to find encouragement and healing through God.

As the voice for "*Joy In The Morning*" for over a decade, Joy successfully blended real life lessons into daily life with God sharing spiritual wisdom and courage from her deeply compassionate heart. If you have ever felt hopeless, helpless and discouraged...don't give up. Joy, His joy has a way of turning sorrow into gladness!

Contact Joy *for women's events and speaking engagements or just to say hello:*

Email: iJoyinspirations@gmail.com

Website: www.iJoyinspirations.com

The Miller Family…nothing missing, nothing broken!

Christopher Charles Miller

1991 – 2005
(Earth Years)

I'm having a blast in Heaven…<u>see</u> <u>you</u> <u>there!</u>

Made in the USA
Charleston, SC
08 April 2013